Developing Intimacy with God

Book Three of the Duncan-Williams Youth Series

Archbishop Nicholas Duncan-Williams

A GOSHEN PUBLISHERS PAPERBACK   VIRGINIA

Developing Intimacy with God
Book Three

ISBN: 978-0-9994003-9-5
Copyright ©2019 Nicolas Duncan-Williams

All rights reserved solely by the author. The author guarantees all contents are original and do not infringe upon the legal rights of any other person or work. No part of this book may be reproduced, shared in a retrieval system, or transmitted in any form or by any means, electronic, mechanical, photocopying, and recording, without prior written permission of the Author/Publisher. Most scriptural quotations are from the King James Version of the Bible.

Published in 2019
by:

GOSHEN PUBLISHERS LLC
P.O. Box 1562
Stephens City, Virginia, USA
www.GoshenPublishers.com

Our books may be purchased in bulk for promotional, educational, or business use. Please email Agents@GoshenPublishers.com.

First Edition 2019

Cover designed by Goshen Publishers LLC

The Duncan-Williams Youth Series seeks, among several others, to bless you in the following ways:

1. Help you totally yield your life and your future to God, trusting and depending wholly on Him;

2. Equip and challenge you to build and maintain a vibrant intimate relationship with God so you can navigate the journey of life more decisively;

3. Help you become a man or woman of prayer, drawing power from your fellowship with God to deal with situations in your life;

4. Get you to pay closer attention to the value of the family of God on earth, so

you can stay with the brethren and not become an easy target of the enemy;

5. Help you identify sin in its forms and resolve to confront sin with the principles and power of God;

6. Dare you to be different in your generation that is heavily influenced by immorality and godlessness, and thereby walk in integrity, honoring God in your life always;

7. Assist you to discover and develop your God-given talents and spiritual gifts by which you can offer acceptable service in the house of God;

8. Help you develop Christian character as the foundation for a future life of

leadership and purpose;

9. Challenge you to share your faith in Christ as per the gospel, and God's power unto salvation without fear, and become a good evangelist for God;

10. Help you know how to draw strength from the holy spirit, stand in the position of authority, and walk in victory in all the issues confronting you as a growing person; and

11. Help you understand and develop healthful habits in relating with the opposite sex, and thereby prepare for a meaningful marriage and family life.

DEVELOPING INTIMACY WITH GOD

BOOK THREE

Other Publications in this series:

- ✓ Book 1: *Beginning with God*
- ✓ Book 2: *Becoming a Strong Christian*
- ✓ Book 4: *Setting Yourself apart unto God*
- ✓ Book 5: *Discovering and Walking in Purpose*

All by Archbishop Nicholas Duncan-Williams

This book belongs to

_____

[Name]

CONTENTS

INTRODUCTION 1

1. GOD DESIRES INTIMACY WITH HIS CHILDREN 5

2. INTIMACY MEANS BECOMING GOD'S FRIEND..................21

3. INTIMACY REQUIRES KNOWING GOD EXPERIENTIALLY.........35

4. INTIMACY MAKES PRAYER CONVERSATIONAL 47

5. WORSHIP: HIGHEST ACTIVITY INTIMACY..........................65

6. YIELDING TO GOD'S WILL...77

INTRODUCTION

In the second book of this series, I taught about the importance of spending time with God. I spoke about prayer and its benefits to the believer. I trust that you were blessed and are growing into a person of prayer. Next in this series, I want to take fellowship with God to another level. Let's talk about intimacy with God.

First, what do we mean when we speak of intimacy? In our ordinary life we know that we have categories or levels of relationship with our peers. Some are acquaintances; we know they are around, and we have some information about them by virtue of the fact we live in the same environment. We do not relate with our acquaintances at the personal level. We know next to little about them, most likely their name and where they live, and the program they are enrolled in at school, and that is all.

At the next level, we have a bit of a personal relationship with people because we meet, and a commonality brings us together. This increases the frequency of our meetings. We discuss those issues of common interest and how they affect us. Sometimes we act like friends and other times we just see each other and move on.

Then we move to the next level with people who are becoming a part of our lives. Such are the people we have opened our lives to, normally one or sometimes two, but they are very few. Three is a crowd.

Of the two, there still may be one to whom you are so close he knows practically everything about you. He has seen you rise and fall, and express joy and sorrow. You can say you know him through and through and can even predict how he will respond to situations. With such a person you have developed intimacy because you share each other's pain and joy. You talk about your fears and doubts. You share your hopes and dreams and expectations for life. You even share your personal weaknesses and try to help each other overcome. You have built such mutual trust that you can defend each other anywhere. Now you have someone with whom you have become intimate.

Intimacy can develop between people of the same sex or between two people of the opposite sex, and the idea is not an erotic relationship. For most young people the mention of intimacy immediately introduces the idea of wanting to have a romantic relationship that leads to getting involved with each other sexually. That is not the intimacy we are talking about here. You can be intimate with someone without getting sexually involved.

Now that you have an idea of what intimacy means, let's see how we can extend this to intimacy with God, your heavenly Father.

1.

GOD DESIRES INTIMACY WITH HIS CHILDREN

God wants you to have an intimate relationship with Him. To this end He has determined that there should be nothing that can separate us from the love He has for us. This means God has set the stage for intimacy to develop between Him and us. He has taken the first step and we must respond positively.

35 *Who shall separate us from the love of Christ? Shall tribulation, or distress, or persecution, or famine, or nakedness, or danger, or sword?*

36 *As it is written,*

"For your sake we are being killed all the day long; we are regarded as sheep to be slaughtered."

37 *No, in all these things we are more than conquerors through him who loved us.*

³⁸ *For I am sure that neither death nor life, nor angels nor rulers, nor things present nor things to come, nor powers,*

³⁹ *nor height nor depth, nor anything else in all creation, will be able to separate us from the love of God in Christ Jesus our Lord.*

Romans 8:35-39

Intimacy with God is not just spending time with God. Without spending time in prayer, you cannot talk about intimacy with God. But intimacy is beyond the act of prayer. Prayer is the communication that can go on in an intimate relationship with God, but prayer, per se, does not constitute intimacy. You can go to God and still maintain a shallow relationship with Him. A typical example is when all you do in prayer is go to God with a shopping list, asking God to provide you with money to pick all the items on the list. That is prayer, but that kind of prayer cannot be described as intimacy. In fact, it cannot promote intimacy.

Being intimate with God means God wants us to know Him as much as He knows us. That goes beyond acquaintance. It even transcends any of the human levels of relationship.

What makes the relationship intimate is the overall quality of the relationship. It means you must put quality in your relationship with God. Certain virtues must be there for intimacy to prevail.

Read the Scriptures below. They all have one thing in common. They all indicate that God wants a higher relationship with us than just being born again.

1   *Ho, every one that thirsteth, come ye to the waters, and he that hath no*

money; come ye, buy, and eat; yea, come, buy wine and milk without money and without price.

2 Wherefore do ye spend money for that which is not bread? and your labour for that which satisfieth not? hearken diligently unto me, and eat ye that which is good, and let your soul delight itself in fatness.

3 Incline your ear, and come unto me: hear, and your soul shall live; and I will make an everlasting covenant with you, even the sure mercies of David.

Isaiah 55:1-3

The Spirit and the Bride say, "Come." And let the one who hears say, "Come." And let the one who is *thirsty come; let the one who desires take the water of life without price.*

Revelation 22:17

Behold, I stand at the door and knock. If anyone hears my voice and opens the door, I will come in to him and eat with him, and he with me.

Revelation 3:20

If you meditate on the passages above, you get an understanding of the extent God wants you to be involved with Him. It goes beyond just giving you a few things for your life on earth.

Read the following passage also and see if you can feel Jesus' heartbeat in the passage. Jesus is like a man whose wife does not stay at home and he has to go looking for her on a daily basis. His wife is all over the place and He is, therefore, constantly searching for her.

37 *O Jerusalem, Jerusalem, the city that kills the prophets and stones those who are sent to it! How often would I have gathered your children together as a hen gathers her brood under her wings, and you were not willing!*

38 *See, your house is left to you desolate.*

39 *For I tell you, you will not see me again, until you say, 'Blessed is he who comes in the name of the Lord.'*

Matthew 23:37-39

God always wants to gather us like a hen gathers her chickens so she can brood over them. If you understand poultry, you know that the period of brooding houses the process that makes eggs hatch into live chickens. Brooding produces life, and that is what God has for you if you become intimate with Him.

King David is one of the few individuals in biblical history who showed a passion for being intimate with God. See if you can learn from this passage the extent of his desire to be intimate with God. He compares his hunger for God with that of a deer looking for water in dry and waterless places. It means that until it finds water, it continues to search for it.

¹ *As a deer pants for flowing streams, so pants my soul for you, O God.*

² *My soul thirsts for God, for the living God. When shall I come and appear before God?*

³ *My tears have been my food day and night, while they say to me all the day long, "Where is your God?"*

⁴ These things I remember, as I pour
    out my soul: how I would go with the
    throng and lead them in procession
    to the house of God with glad shouts
    and songs of praise, a multitude
    keeping festival.

Psalm 42:1-4

In the same way, God expects us to desire to be with Him as He has opened the door for us to come in.

¹ O God, you are my God; earnestly I
    seek you; my soul thirsts for you; my
    flesh faints for you, as in a dry and
    weary land where there is no water.

² So I have looked upon you in the
    sanctuary, beholding your power
    and glory.

³ Because your steadfast love is better
    than life, my lips will praise you.

4   So I will bless you as long as I live; in your name I will lift up my hands.

5   My soul will be satisfied as with fat and rich food, and my mouth will praise you with joyful lips,

6   when I remember you upon my bed, and meditate on you in the watches of the night;

7   for you have been my help, and in the shadow of your wings I will sing for joy.

8   My soul clings to you; your right hand upholds me.

Psalm 63:1-8

When you know someone very well and the person knows you very well, it becomes a fertile ground to develop intimacy. How thirsty are you for God? King David is not talking about naming and claiming. He is longing for God Himself.

Let us see what we can learn from the Apostle Paul also concerning intimacy. If you are intimate with someone, it means it is difficult for something to stand in the way of your relationship with that person. All other things become secondary. That is what the Apostle Paul tried to convey in his letter to the church at Philippi.

> 7   *But whatever gain I had, I counted as loss for the sake of Christ*
>
> 8   *Indeed, I count everything as loss because of the surpassing worth of knowing Christ Jesus my Lord. For his sake I have suffered the loss of all things and count them as rubbish, in order that I may gain Christ*
>
> 9   *and be found in him, not having a righteousness of my own that comes from the law, but that which comes through faith in Christ, the*

> righteousness from God that depends on faith—
>
> 10 that I may know him and the power of his resurrection, and may share his sufferings, becoming like him in his death,
>
> 11 that by any means possible I may attain the resurrection from the dead.
>
> Philippians 3:7-11

You have to understand the person making this statement. Paul was not an ordinary citizen by the standards of the day. He was a pharisee, a teacher of the law. He was intelligent; yet he counted all those things as rubbish compared with the relationship he wanted to have with Jesus.

That is a passion for intimacy at its highest level. Sometimes one wonders the things that make people play down their relationship with Jesus. The apostle Paul did not fall in that category. Jesus meant everything to him. After all that he did, he was still longing to know Jesus more.

> **It is more virtuous to yearn more for the Giver, not the gifts, because the Giver is always far above any gift He can give you.**

As a young person with all the types of pressure on you, you have to identify those things that could stand in the way of your intimacy with God and deal with them. Dealing with them means you see them as secondary, with Jesus being first.

If it means that in situations where you are confronted with making a choice between any of them and what Jesus expects of you, the decision will go in favor of what Jesus expects of you.

Things that could stand in the way of my intimacy with God

_____

_____

_____

_____

_____

_____

_____

_____

2.

INTIMACY MEANS BECOMING GOD'S

FRIEND

There can be no intimacy with anyone if the person is not your friend. This means that to become intimate with God, you and God must become friends. It is not a strange thing for a human to become God's friend. There are instances in the Bible that point to that. The first we can look at is that of Abraham. Here's the story:

> 17 The LORD said, "Shall I hide from Abraham what I am about to do,
>
> 18 seeing that Abraham shall surely become a great and mighty nation, and all the nations of the earth shall be blessed in him?
>
> 19 For I have chosen him, that he may command his children and his household after him to keep the way of the LORD by doing righteousness and justice, so that the LORD may

bring to Abraham what he has promised him."

20 Then the LORD said, "Because the outcry against Sodom and Gomorrah is great and their sin is very grave,

21 I will go down to see whether they have done altogether according to the outcry that has come to me. And if not, I will know."

Genesis 18:17-21

Hear God speaking about Abraham, reasoning within Himself why He should not tell Abraham what He intended to do with Sodom and Gomorrah. If you have something you consider very important to you, the only person you immediately want to discuss it with is your friend. This is someone you trust, and you think can handle the issue well. It may look like God wanted Abraham's mind concerning Sodom and Gomorrah. Look beyond that. See how spontaneous God made the decision to tell Abraham of His intentions. It is only someone you have intimacy with that you ask their opinion concerning very serious issues.

Following the story, you know there was a long conversation between God and Abraham where Abraham was trying to reason with God to think it through again. As the story goes, Sodom and Gomorrah could not meet the lowest bid that God would have considered, as per Abraham's negotiation.

Note also that God established that He had a certain level of trust in Abraham. It was not only Abraham who trusted God. God also trusted that Abraham would teach his children the ways of God. That was why God was not ashamed to see Abraham as His friend.

Later in the friendship, God made a request of Abraham to sacrifice his only son, Isaac. Abraham yielded to God and God intervened and provided a lamb for the sacrifice. Yielding to God is one of the characteristics of the intimate relationship. You yield to one another. The difference here is that God does not yield to what we say because He knows much more than we know, and He has more control over all the issues involved than we do.

The second example in the Bible that describes God's intimate relationship with men is recorded in the book of Numbers and it involves God's friendship with Moses, His servant.

1   *Miriam and Aaron spoke against Moses because of the Cushite woman whom he had married, for he had married a Cushite woman.*

2   *And they said, "Has the LORD indeed spoken only through Moses? Has he not spoken through us also?" And the LORD heard it.*

3   Now the man Moses was very meek, more than all people who were on the face of the earth.

4   And suddenly the L ORD *said to Moses and to Aaron and Miriam,* "Come out, you three, to the tent of meeting." *And the three of them came out.*

5   *And the* L ORD *came down in a pillar of cloud and stood at the entrance of the tent and called Aaron and Miriam, and they both came forward.*

6   *And he said,* "Hear my words: If there is a prophet among you, I the L ORD *make myself known to him in a vision; I speak with him in a dream.*

7   *Not so with my servant Moses. He is faithful in all my house.*

8   *With him I speak mouth to mouth,*
clearly, and not in riddles, and he
beholds the form of the LORD. *Why*
then were you not afraid to speak
against my servant Moses?"

9   *And the anger of the* LORD *was*
kindled against them, and he
departed.

Numbers 12:1-9

The point of interest here is not the gossip of Aaron and Miriam and the punishment God issued out to Miriam. It is about God's regard for Moses, the man He had called to carry out His task. God treasured the friendship He had built with Moses. See how He put it. God said He speaks with men in riddles and in dreams, but with Moses He spoke with him face to face. That shows the level of the relationship Moses had with God. God was saying to Miriam and Aaron, "You better not touch My friend". I am sure they got the message, because there is no recording of such an incident again.

What we have to understand today is that God is constantly seeking relationship with us beyond just asking Him to do things for us. It is beyond bless me O Lord. We should be saying, "Lord You can have me."

It is fair to say that over the generations, God had always sought such relationship with His children. I am very sure there were several other servants of God that He considered as friends. Did He not describe King David as the man after His heart?

Can you think of yourself as God's friend? It does not matter your age. As a matter of fact, He would rather have you at an early age before you get contaminated with too many of the elements of the current world. If you make yourself available, God knows how to both initiate the friendship and how to sustain it. You simply must be willing.

Let's consider our Lord Jesus as well. When He was on earth as a man, Jesus called 12 disciples to be with Him as His support team, and also as the people into whose hands He would commit the destiny of the world. Within the twelve disciples, there were three of them that He spent more time than the others – Peter, John, and James. He must have had a reason for developing a more intimate friendship with these three. Is it strange that John, Peter and James wrote portions of the New Testament? These learned more of Jesus than the rest of the twelve. They enjoyed a greater level of intimacy with the Master.

What else would make Peter rebuke Jesus for going to Jerusalem when He knew they were looking for Him to kill Him. Peter was so concerned about His Master and Friend, he did not want anything to happen to Him. Jesus also, at a point in time, referred to His disciples as His friends.

12 *This is my commandment, that you love one another as I have loved you.*

13 *Greater love has no one than this, that someone lay down his life for his friends.*

14 *You are my friends if you do what I command you.*

15 *No longer do I call you servants, for the servant does not know what his master is doing; but I have called you friends, for all that I have heard from my Father I have made known to you.*

John 15:12-15

Jesus called His disciples His friends because He had told them all that the Father had told Him, even though they did not fully understand all of it. Just like God shared with Abraham, His friend, what He wanted to do with Sodom and Gomorrah, Jesus told His friends what the Father wanted to do for humanity. Sharing is critical to friendship and intimacy and that is what we are seeing here.

God wants you to become His friend. You have to be ready to trust God and be ready to open your heart to all that He wants you to know.

Today, I am ready to trust God and I open my heart to all that He wants me to know.

_____

[DATE]

3.

INTIMACY REQUIRES KNOWING GOD EXPERIENTIALLY

Let me explain the difference between knowing God and knowing the Scriptures. It is good to know what the Bible says, but that is no guarantee that one is intimate with God. Too many people have a mental knowledge of what is written in the Scriptures. Even the devil knows what is written in the Scriptures, but we know he does not have a relationship with God.

You can know all the Scriptures about the love of God and His commitment to you and your welfare, but that does not necessarily mean you are intimate with God. Intimacy has to be cultivated.

We know God when we experience Him in all His attributes. The Scriptures help us to understand God, but we must experience Him practically. If you read about the names the Hebrews gave God, each of them came out of an experience they had with Him. Abraham, for example, knew God as the God who provides because He provided a lamb for the sacrifice when God told him to not touch his son, Isaac.

Experiential knowledge of God contributes to intimacy. What we encounter in our daily walk with Him through life's situations makes an indelible mark, which no man can erase from our minds and hearts.

It is by these that we come to know God very well. The more we know Him experientially, the more intimate we become with Him. The more you know God, the more you trust Him, especially as you see Him fighting your battles and giving you victory on every hand. When you trust God, it means a lot. You yield absolutely to Him and His plans and purposes for your life. The more you trust Him the more you want to be with Him. Trust helps you become more open with God and telling Him all about yourself. Trusting Him makes you give up all that you think is important to you and, in their place, look up to Him in all things.

Take King David, for example, who knew God through experience:

1. **Killing the lion and the bear in the field while taking care of his father's sheep;**

2. **Killing the giant who blasphemed the name of Jehovah night after night with no response from the army of Israel;**

3. **Seeing God's hand protect him from King Saul, with God's hand upon him when he was a vagabond in the earth running away from the same king Saul; and**

4. **The time he became king and all that God did for him, including forgiving him when he sinned against God by adultery and murder.**

David had a lot in his repertoire regarding who God is and what God will do for anyone.

Does it surprise you then that He was the greatest worshipper of all times? David never struggled to worship God like we do today. Worshipping God came to him like drinking water. He did not need to squeeze his face or squint or do some of the things we do in church to show we are worshipping. He just did a recap of his encounters with God and turned them into praise unto God.

Consider one of David's praises for God's Deliverance:

> ¹ *And David spake unto the Lord the words of this song in the day that the Lord had delivered him out of*

the hand of all his enemies, and out
of the hand of Saul:

2   And he said, The Lord is my rock, and
my fortress, and my deliverer;

3   The God of my rock; in him will I
trust: he is my shield, and the horn of
my salvation, my high tower, and my
refuge, my saviour; thou savest me
from violence.

4   I will call on the Lord, who is worthy
to be praised: so shall I be saved
from mine enemies.

5   When the waves of death compassed
me, the floods of unGodly men made
me afraid;

6   The sorrows of hell compassed me
about; the snares of death prevented
me;

7 In my distress I called upon the Lord,
and cried to my God: and he did hear
my voice out of his temple, and my
cry did enter into his ears.

8 Then the earth shook and trembled;
the foundations of heaven moved
and shook, because he was wroth.

9 There went up a smoke out of his
nostrils, and fire out of his mouth
devoured: coals were kindled by it.

2 Samuel 22:1-9

The king knew the God who delivers one from his enemies. Spend time reading the psalms and you can see a comprehensive recording of David's experiences of God's attributes. That is how he became intimate with God.

The more time you spend with God on a consistent basis, the better you know what He likes and what He does not like, and the more you know what He has for you. Time spent with God is not restricted to the early mornings when you wake up and spend an hour or two in prayer. It goes beyond that. It graduates into the day even as you engage in the affairs of this life.

The psalmist wrote concerning being in God's presence and said

> 1 *He who dwells in the shelter of the Most High will abide in the shadow of the Almighty.*
>
> 2 *I will say to the LORD, "My refuge and my fortress, my God, in whom I trust."*

> Psalm 91:1-2

Your dwelling place is where you live. So, the psalmist is not talking about a temporary place like you come to church or attend a Christian gathering or shut yourself up in your room. He means that practically everywhere you are, you can be in God's presence. It is this abiding in His presence that produces intimacy.

It is the same psalmist who acknowledged that God is everywhere, and he cannot run away from God's presence. This is how he put it:

> 7   Where shall I go from your Spirit? Or where shall I flee from your presence?
>
> 8   If I ascend to heaven, you are there! If I make my bed in Sheol, you are there!
>
> 9   If I take the wings of the morning and dwell in the uttermost parts of the sea,
>
> 10   even there your hand shall lead me, and your right hand shall hold me.
>
> 11   If I say, "Surely the darkness shall cover me, and the light about me be night,"

¹² *even the darkness is not dark to you;*

the night is bright as the day, for

darkness is as light with you

Psalm 139:7-12

If you put the two Scriptures from King David together with several others he wrote, you get the picture of what it means to be close with God. You can be in God's presence any day, any time, and under any situation you find yourself.

When you are conscious of God's presence wherever you are, you expect Him to show up in your circumstances; and He does. That is how you build a repertoire of testimonies of His goodness. The more personal testimonies you have in your experience with God, the more intimate you end up becoming with God.

4.

INTIMACY MAKES PRAYER

CONVERSATIONAL

The average Christian understands and operates prayer with a request paradigm. For most people, prayer is asking God for things. It includes making declarations and decrees for the things that they believe will make their lives on earth more meaningful. For some, it is an opportunity to receive more anointing to demonstrate power everywhere they go. For whatever motivates people to pray, the format has always been asking to get something from God.

That mode of prayer looks like taking a shopping list to God and as He answers them, checking the items as you do when you buy them. That has been some people's experience and there is absolutely nothing wrong with that. There is a place for that, and God acknowledges and endorses it. He responds to those kinds of prayers when they come from a sincere heart.

Intimacy with God, however, goes beyond a prayer list with intercessors being paid to ask God for things on behalf of people. We give a variety of names to the prayer teams in churches like prayer warriors, prayer force, and the like. They enter prayer with the goal of taking things. That is much of the possessive form of prayer. They have to go beyond that.

Even with your earthly father, do you have only an asking relationship with him? In other words, do you communicate with your father only when you want him to give you something you desperately need? Don't you occasionally sit and chat with your dad, talking about everything else around you without ask him for something?

I am sure that for most young people, it is not a common experience to simply have a conversation with their earthly fathers for the sake of having a chat to know and understand their dads better.

Such people may struggle with the conversational mode when praying in their closets.

Personal Conversations with My Heavenly Father

What goes into the long periods that people spend in God's presence, particularly in their closets all by themselves? Do they spend three hours in God's presence only asking Him things they want to do for them? That certainly must be an uninteresting time. It would be like you're doing all the lecturing and God does all the listening; and all He has to do is simply listen to you talk the whole period.

Let's find out what we can learn from the early days of creation. The following passage suggests that God had conversations with Adam and Eve on a continual basis. It was a two-way communication. It was not Adam talking the whole time and neither was God speaking the whole time.

It was an interactive communication between God and the first humans He had created.

> 8 And they heard the voice of the Lord God walking in the garden in the cool of the day: and Adam and his wife hid themselves from the presence of the Lord God amongst the trees of the garden.
>
> 9 And the Lord God called unto Adam, and said unto him, Where art thou?
>
> 10 And he said, I heard thy voice in the garden, and I was afraid, because I was naked; and I hid myself.
>
> 11 And he said, Who told thee that thou wast naked? Hast thou eaten of the tree, whereof I commanded thee that thou shouldest not eat?

12 *And the man said, The woman whom thou gavest to be with me, she gave me of the tree, and I did eat.*

13 *And the Lord God said unto the woman, What is this that thou hast done? And the woman said, The serpent beguiled me, and I did eat.*

Genesis 3:8-13

Even when Adam and Eve had eaten the forbidden fruit, God still had a two-way communication with them. When you have a two-way communication with someone, the arrangement is that you speak while the other person listens and vice versa.

Having conversations with God in your quiet moments is the greatest form of communication that promotes intimacy. Most young people and, in fact, most adult Christians are yet to get to that point. The kind of communication God had with

Adam and Eve before the Fall in the Garden of Eden is definitely the blueprint for intimacy.

It must be the same experience Jesus had with the Father in those forty days and nights He spent fasting in the wilderness before the official launching of His ministry. I am sure they were talking about where the world is going, affirming that Jesus had come at the appointed time.

They probably were also talking about the enemy and what he had been doing to the sons of men since the creation and affirming that Jesus was on earth to bring to an end the devil's work in the lives of people on earth. They surely must have been in some kind of conversation to be occupied for forty days and forty nights.

Pause and ask yourself the question: "What do I talk about with God in the moments of being alone with Him?" If you are unable to freely say what you are going through with God, then your relationship is not yet intimate.

What do you talk with God about? He has given you a clue in His message through the Prophet Isaiah about one example of a conversation you can have with God in those intimate fellowships:

> 15 *And when ye spread forth your hands, I will hide mine eyes from you: yea, when ye make many prayers, I will not hear: your hands are full of blood.*
>
> 16 *Wash you, make you clean; put away the evil of your doings from before mine eyes; cease to do evil;*
>
> 17 *Learn to do well; seek judgment, relieve the oppressed, judge the fatherless, plead for the widow.*
>
> 18 *Come now, and let us reason together, saith the LORD: though*

your sins be as scarlet, they shall be
as white as snow; though they be red
like crimson, they shall be as wool.

Isaiah 1:15-18

It is only with someone with whom you are intimate that you can share your weaknesses and the troubling life you are experiencing because of that weakness. You can talk with God about your personal weaknesses. No one else understands your struggles in this life.

Men may ridicule you and say all manner of evil things against you. That is how far men can go, very often not offering any help, simply condemning both you and whatever shows from your weaknesses.

In your intimate fellowship with God you have the liberty to pour your heart out to Him concerning the personal struggles you go through in your Christian life. Talk to God about that sin that constantly flaws you and looks like would keep you in permanent bondage.

There is this song that says,

Tell it unto Jesus, He's the One who cares,

Tell it unto Jesus, He'll all your burdens bear,

or maybe if you told me I would not understand

but you can tell it unto Jesus, for Jesus understands.

[Author Unknown]

God is ready to hear about it all; and He is ready and willing to get you out of any personal trouble. Get a true picture of what I am talking about from no other person than the Psalmist himself once again:

> ¹ *Have mercy upon me, O God, according to thy lovingkindness:*

according unto the multitude of thy tender mercies blot out my transgressions.

2 Wash me throughly from mine iniquity, and cleanse me from my sin.

3 For I acknowledge my transgressions: and my sin is ever before me.

4 Against thee, thee only, have I sinned, and done this evil in thy sight: that thou mightest be justified when thou speakest, and be clear when thou judgest.

5 Behold, I was shapen in iniquity; and in sin did my mother conceive me.

6 Behold, thou desirest truth in the inward parts: and in the hidden part thou shalt make me to know wisdom.

7 *Purge me with hyssop, and I shall be clean: wash me, and I shall be whiter than snow.*

8 *Make me to hear joy and gladness; that the bones which thou hast broken may rejoice.*

9 *Hide thy face from my sins, and blot out all mine iniquities.*

10 *Create in me a clean heart, O God; and renew a right spirit within me.*

11 *Cast me not away from thy presence; and take not thy holy spirit from me.*

12 *Restore unto me the joy of thy salvation; and uphold me with thy free spirit.*

Psalm 51:1-12

I think there is a lot we can learn from King David regarding intimacy with God. The same David whom we found worshipping God in those happy moments comes to God this time crying over his weakness and the trouble it brought to him. It is believed that he wrote this prayer after he had committed adultery with Uriah's wife and arranged to have Uriah killed in battle. Before whom can he go with this kind of mess, apart from Him with whom he had an intimate relationship?

1. Seek clarity on God's purpose for your life. Create an open conversation for God to minister to you and thereby help you figure out what He wants you to spend your life doing. You can talk with Him about your passion for life and have Him affirm or redirect your concerning it.

2. There is a particular Scripture that you have read over and over but cannot properly interpret it. God is willing to illuminate your mind on the passage and also erase any

errors you have picked in your struggle to understand that Scripture.

3. Meditate on creation. Creation reveals the character of God. Chat with God about the wonder of creation, His power that has held the entire creation until today, including the immaculate order and harmony in the universe, and what it means to you. Talk also about things you don't understand about His creation.

4. Pick up a conversation with God about some of life's issues like people suffering, and some prayers not getting answered or taking long before the answer shows up.

5. Sometimes people share their hurts, disappointments, and the things that made their day unpleasant. This is typical of sharing

your emotions with someone you are intimate with.

6. You also have opportunity to share what pleasant experiences you had during the day, those moments when you felt you were on top of the world because of some breakthrough that came your way.

Intimacy with God provides you support for those moments when you may even condemn yourself because of some grievous sin you committed in men's eyes. Where you relate with men superficially, you can be as open with God as you need, once you establish enough intimacy with Him. This is the beauty of an intimate relationship.

As the name suggests, a conversational prayer is founded on the premise that God wants to talk back to you in those

moments you spend before Him. It deviates from the one-way traffic where we do all the talking and God is expected to listen and do what we ask Him.

The conversational prayer that promotes intimacy with God requires that you also know how God speaks with you. Hearing from God is a topic I will like to treat in another book. It is a bit delicate because today we have a lot of people claiming to have heard from God when that is not the case.

God speaks to each of us differently. Very few people hear God's audible voice like a man speaks with another man. However, God ministers to us through our spirit. When your spirit is sensitive to the Holy Spirit, you will catch a glimpse of the Holy Spirit's whispers to your spirit and it helps in the intimacy conversation I am talking about here.

5.

WORSHIP:

HIGHEST ACTIVITY INTIMACY

Of all that takes place in your closet with God toward intimacy, worship is the highest. Unfortunately worship today has been restricted to singing songs in a slow tempo in church. What happens when one enters his closet and there is no music in there? What if you cannot trust yourself to sing nicely to God anywhere; church or your home? Does it mean you cannot worship? Far from that! You can worship God without singing.

When we talk about worship, let us not limit it to just singing songs written by gospel musicians using their music talent and their creativity to compose songs that talk about God. The songs that we learn and sing, help us in worship when, by ourselves, we struggle to say something to God. Why do we struggle? It is because we seem to have nothing to tell God.

Worship typically finds expression in telling God what we know about Him. Each time we speak or sing, and the words that we say or sing are telling who God is and what he has done for us, we are engaged in worship. This means without the song of gospel musicians we can still worship.

Let's take a close look at Hannah's song again:

1 *And Hannah prayed, and said, My heart rejoiceth in the Lord, mine horn is exalted in the Lord: my mouth is enlarged over mine enemies; because I rejoice in thy salvation.*

2 *There is none holy as the LORD: for there is none beside thee: neither is there any rock like our God.*

3 *Talk no more so exceeding proudly; let not arrogancy come out of your*

mouth: for the LORD is a God of knowledge, and by him actions are weighed.

4 The bows of the mighty men are broken, and they that stumbled are girded with strength.

5 They that were full have hired out themselves for bread; and they that were hungry ceased: so that the barren hath born seven; and she that hath many children is waxed feeble.

6 The LORD killeth, and maketh alive: he bringeth down to the grave, and bringeth up.

7 The LORD maketh poor, and maketh rich: he bringeth low, and lifteth up.

8 He raiseth up the poor out of the dust, and lifteth up the beggar from the dunghill, to set them among

princes, and to make them inherit
the throne of glory: for the pillars of
the earth are the LORD's, and he hath
set the world upon them.

1 Samuel 2:1-8

Hannah sang this song of praise when God heard her prayer and gave her the son she had requested. You can tell from the prayer that she was actually telling God what she has learned of God in her situation. She experienced the God who silences the wicked, who raises the poor into wealth, who makes the barren a mother of seven, etc.

These were her declarations of God. She could continue on and on and on because she had been praying for years for this child. Hannah's experience increased her repertoire of who God is and what God can do, and that is the substance of her worship.

I have said quite a lot about King David. He is an Old Testament saint who worshipped God at all times. The psalms are full of worship. They are full of David's expression of what he learned of God in the circumstances and situations he encountered.

Have you ever thought that you could also sing your songs or declare what God is to you without singing? This is the greatest thing that happens in intimacy with God.

When you go into God's presence in your closet for example, simply allow the Holy Spirit to lead you. I can always recall from where God picked me. My personal life is a testimony of God's goodness. It is full of the manifestation of God's characteristics: His protective power; His delivering power; His love that provides for His children; and His sovereignty in lifting up people from a low estate to a high position in this life.

Because of what God did to me that has brought me to where I am in life today, I should not struggle to worship. I simply play back my life to God in those moments and let God know I really appreciate what he did to ensure that I did not go to hell in the first place, and also that I am not a disgrace in life because of His grace.

Yes, God's grace was enough to spare me disgrace in this life. These are facts about my life that I cannot forget. I am not ashamed to proclaim that it is God who has made me what I am today. I do not struggle to remember all these. Each time I get into His presence, these form a great part of my fellowship with Him.

The awe I have of God in my heart as a result of these experiences constitutes my foundation for worship. In that intimate relationship with Him, I simply recount all these before Him with a heart of gratitude.

You may be young and have not lived many years yet. Nevertheless, I am sure you have had your own portion of experiences that affirmed to you that God is the One who has brought you this far. Pause and assemble all these experiences. The more you assemble them the more you identify God's characteristics and His attributes.

If you do this prayerfully and factually, you will be amazed at what you have learned of God in these experiences. So, you see you have knowledge of God that is beyond reading the Scriptures. It is this knowledge you have of God that you express to God in worship each time you go before Him.

My experiences that affirm to me that God is the One who has brought me this far

1. _____

2. _____

3. _____

4. _____

5. _____

6. _____

6.

YIELDING TO GOD'S WILL

One of the characteristics of intimacy is yielding your will to God. As you wait in His presence, just the two of you, you acknowledge that your life is of no significance except it conforms to what God wants it to be. In other words, in His presence you lose your will totally into His. That was Jesus' experience in the Garden of Gethsemane.

> 35 *And going a little farther, he fell on the ground and prayed that, if it were possible, the hour might pass from him.*
>
> 36 *And he said, "Abba, Father, all things are possible for you. Remove this cup from me. Yet not what I will, but what you will*

Mark 14:35-36

Jesus, in the garden, saw how awful death looks. The whole picture of what He was going to face was made bare before Him. What was also made bare to Him was the picture of you and me and several others on the face of the earth coming back to God as a result of going to the cross to suffer shame and death. Jesus had a choice to make: either go back to heaven without going to the cross; or facing death on the cross. Guess what? He chose the latter. He chose God's will. That simply is what yielding is about.

As young person you have been dreaming of what you want to become. It is possible this started when you were in primary school or even earlier. The experts think that most of what people want to become when they are young usually change as they grow and reality hits them.

At a certain stage in your life, you are the one who makes the important decisions for your life. Even your parents only act as guides. Sometimes they even back off altogether for fear of being branded as interferers.

When you get to the age of accountability and you become responsible for your own actions, God begins to call you to yield to Him. What happens when God comes into the equation? Does God interfere with your plans for your life?

He does not. God is careful to not force you to make decisions. Sometimes He simply watches us make even the wrong decisions after ignoring the several promptings by the Holy Spirit. He always knows we will realize we are wrong and come back. What you have to appreciate is that in your relationship with God, your will is very important. Even in the things that God speaks to you, He still waits for you to commit your will to them so He can make them happen in your life.

Yielding to God shows that you trust Him to manage your life. When you yield to God, He takes you up and the result blows the human mind.

This is an experience all youth should have. Some people yield their lives to God at a latter age in their lives. Then they realize they should have done it earlier because of the bitter experiences they went through. What happens if you yield very early in life? The blessings are countless and mind blowing. You have a long life of exciting experiences with God. He is able to reveal so much of His plans and purposes to you and then works with you daily to make these materialize at the times He has appointed.

No one yields their lives to God and comes out lame. You never lose; you gain a lot. What scares people is that they are afraid God will demand they give up some lifestyle, or something they cherish way above God.

Make yourself a checklist to evaluate how much of your life is truly yielded to God

1. What thoughts and opinions about life issues are you holding on to that you know deep in your heart that you have to give up in order for your Christian life to be pleasing in the sight of God?

_____

_____

_____

_____

2. What attitudes have you unconsciously cultivated over the years that God wants you to give up, but you still hold on to them?

Remember that not all of the attitudes we cultivate out of the pressures and circumstances of this life are helpful to us. Some really harm us in the long run.

_____

_____

_____

_____

3. What behaviors have you developed that do not present you as a Christian before your peers that God wants you to give up? You are not passive when it comes to developing behaviors. The behaviors you permit are the ones that will identify you.

_____

_____

_____

_____

4. What have your parents registered their objections to in your life, reminding you that as a child of God you cannot continue in those things; yet, you are holding on to them because your friends say those are cool?

_____

_____

_____

_____

I encourage to never be scared about yielding to God. When you sing the song, "All to Jesus I surrender," you have to be serious and mean it from the bottom of your heart. Some sing it for the sake of singing. Don't be like them. Sing with all the sincerity it deserves and be open to giving up something if God impresses it on your heart or you read it from His word.

www.ingramcontent.com/pod-product-compliance
Lightning Source LLC
Chambersburg PA
CBHW071820020426
42331CB00007B/1569